DEGAS

THE PAINTED GESTURE

CONTENTS

First published in the United States in 1994 by
Chelsea House Publishers.

© 1992 by Casterman, Tournai

3 5 7 9 8 6 4 2

ISBN 0-7910-2809-7

ART FOR CHILDREN

DEGAS
THE PAINTED GESTURE

By Jacqueline Loumaye

Illustrated by Nadine Massart

Translated by John Goodman

CHELSEA HOUSE PUBLISHERS
NEW YORK • PHILADELPHIA

Greetings parents!

It's the start of the school year, a good time to make resolutions.

To study, to work—that goes without saying; but why not also to discover, to work, to imagine, to have fun? I propose to open an art studio next week for budding draftsmen and tinkerers, for lovers of forms and colors and museum visits.

I hope the idea will interest and excite your children.

Thanks in advance, dear parents, for your confidence in me.

Cordially,
William Cocagne

What a great invitation, this letter I found on the table in our living room when I got home! The year was getting off to a good start; there was as much talk of art and field trips as of rules and lessons! I surely don't need to tell you I was super-enthusiastic from the start. Fortunately, my parents were, too.

"Now you won't need to draw in the margins of your notebooks all the time!" they said to me.

So I signed up for the first visit to the Orsay Museum the following Wednesday. There were eight of us.

"Not bad for starters," William murmured distractedly.

We introduced ourselves. There was Theodore, who wore glasses, Oliver with frizzy hair, Charlotte the short, Laura the blonde, three others, and myself.

"We'll get along just fine!" said William.

As we were about to enter this museum in Paris in a former train station, he said to us:

"The entire artistic heritage of the second half of the nineteenth century and the beginning of the twentieth is gathered together here: sculpture, painting, photography, drawing, and even literature and music."

But that particular day we were going to discover work by painters. The conservative ones who respected the rules of their predecessors and then the modern ones who were determined to express themselves freely, to paint reality—above all the impression it makes on us.

"They're known as the Impressionists," said Theodore with the glasses.

"Exactly! They were the first to break with the old school of painting. But let's not waste any more time. The best way to understand is to see for yourself."

On the lower floor, in rooms that were rather dark, we saw portraits, goddesses, scenes of daily life, and landscapes. The colors were not very bright, but the works were still beautiful. William wanted to give us some idea of the "classic" art of the period, but we didn't stay too long. On the upper floor, how clear everything had become! Sunlight, blue skies, and flowers were everywhere! It was like a trip to the country!

"Here we discover the impressionist palette," explained William. "Do you see the difference? Clear colors, a vibrant light, and fewer outlines. Sometimes the subject even disappears! There's nothing but color spreading across the canvas like a rainbow from earth to sky. Other painters, like Van Gogh, Cezanne, and Gauguin, after having used impressionist techniques, would find new and different ways of expressing themselves. For great painters rarely remain within the confines of a school."

"Like us!" I said. "One can learn lots of things outside the classroom."

That must have put William in a good humor, for we started to have more and more fun.

"And now, who is your favorite painter?" William asked at the end of the visit.

Can you guess who got almost all our votes? Degas! Does that surprise you? There were a lot of interesting artists, of course: Manet, Monet, Renoir. But William's imitations of Edgar Degas grumbling into his beard and his yawning models scratching their backs, acted out in front of the canvases, made us laugh hard. And then we liked the subjects: horses, musicians, dancers . . .

"We could do a whole set of studio sessions on Degas!" proposed William. But first we must situate him in his own time. So when we next get together I'll tell you his story."

That might have been boring. But not with William, who arrived at our first studio class the following Wednesday in top hat and striped vest.

Conclusion of an Arabesque, 1877. Diluted oil and pastel, 2 feet 2 inches × 1 foot 3 inches.

Self Portrait, sometimes called ***Degas with a Charcoal-Holder***, 1855. Oil on canvas, 2 feet 8 inches × 2 feet 1 inch.

Hilaire de Gas, Edgar's grandfather, emigrated to Italy during the French revolution. In Naples he founded a bank and married a young woman from that city. But his son, Auguste de Gas, returned to Paris, where he established a branch of the bank and married Celestine Musson, who was of Creole origin. They had five children. Edgar, born in 1834, was the eldest. But when Edgar was 13 his mother died. This left a great void in the household. His father never remarried. Edgar kept his mother's wedding gown his whole life.

As an adolescent, his father took him to visit the collectors who were among his friends, but there was nothing as yet to suggest Edgar would become a painter.

At school he was a good student and excelled in drawing.

As the eldest son, he was expected to take over his father's business. So he entered law school. At the same time, he took drawing classes and copied works in the Louvre. He secretly dreamed of becoming an artist.

Before long his father permitted him to study with Louis Lamothe, a student of Ingres, at the School of Fine Arts. His law career was over before it started.

In 1855, thanks to a friend of his father's, the collector Valpincon, Degas met Ingres himself, whom he much admired. "I paint", he had uttered tentatively. "I'm just starting out and my father is encouraging me. What do you think?"

The great Ingres leaned over Edgar's work and said to him: "It's good, young man. But make lines. Many lines. Both from memory and after nature."

Edgar never forgot this advice. He was 21. He made his decision. From that point forward he signed with the single word "Degas," which would be his name as a painter. The classes he was taking weren't sufficient. As often as possible, he went to the Louvre, where he made copies of the old masters, especially those from the Italian fifteenth century.

In 1856 he took his first trip to Italy. There he continued to study the old masters who had interested him in Paris: Ghirlandaio, Mantegna, Perugino, and Piero della Francesca. He met the painter Gustave Moreau, who taught him many painting techniques that would later prove useful to him. He also applied himself to the art of portraiture, having many models [to hand] in the family members he had met. He also executed a series of self portraits that evidence his growing mastery. After two years in Italy, he returned to Paris. He left his father's apartment for a studio in the Rue de Laval; he would live in this same neighborhood until his death.

Degas, circa the 1850s.

Beginning in 1860, Degas' life took an important new turn. He abandoned classic, historical painting to study scenes from daily life. To be sure, he had already painted horses and was becoming interested in dancers, but his introduction to Manet decided the matter. Degas would be his ally in the first battles of the ancients against the moderns.

In 1863, 4,000 works by young artists were refused by the official Salon exhibition. They were shown in the "Salon des Refuses" (Salon of the Refused), where Manet exhibited *Picnic on the Grass*, which angered the critics. In 1865 Manet provoked another scandal with his *Olympia*, but he had become the leader of an entire group of young artists: Monet, Renoir, Cezanne . . . They came to be called "Manet's gang."

They all gathered at the Café Guerbois, where discussions were heated. Degas wanted to impose his own ideas. Manet nicknamed him "the great aesthetician." Then the war of 1870 broke out and everyone was separated. But an artistic movement had been born, one that would be baptized "Impressionism" in 1874, on the basis of a painting by Monet entitled *Impression, Sunrise*. This happened during a sensational exhibition mounted in the studio of the photographer Nadar.

But eventually Degas broke with the Impressionists. He preferred the term "independents," with its air of opposition. The Impressionists were determined to paint sunlit landscapes executed in the open air. They blurred all the contours! As for Degas, he hated the country. He preferred to paint inside, in his studio with its artificial light. "If I were the government, I'd send an army brigade to keep watch on these people who do landscapes directly from nature!" he declared. And again: "Doesn't one have everything necessary to make all the landscapes in the world with just a few paints and three old brushes, without ever leaving home?" He always gave priority to drawing over color, for it was the study of movement that fascinated him. He closely followed the evolution of photography. The work of Nadar and especially the British photographer Edward Muybridge, who worked with horses, were a great influence on him beginning around 1878–1880.

When William stopped talking, we had the impression that Degas was among us. We really wanted to know more. Then someone said: "We could make a newspaper about Degas and the nineteenth century!"

William promised us books, documents, and assistance. He even assured me that we could draw . . . in a notebook devoted to art. Things were starting well!

We were already looking forward to our next meeting. When the day arrived, our teacher brought a large reproduction of a painting that astonished us.

"Is that really a Degas?" said Oliver with annoyance. "There isn't a horse in sight."

"And no dancers," added Charlotte.

"It's not very impressionist."

"Certainly not, Damian. This family portrait dates from Degas' youth, when his ambition was to produce a large composition in the tradition of masters like Ingres, Van Dyck, and Valázquez that would be accepted for the official Salon exhibition. It is a masterpiece of its kind, but it did not meet with success. The public found it revolutionary and scandalous—because of small 'errors' that were felt to be unforgivable in an official portrait but that already announced the mature Degas."

"I see one!" said Sarah, blushing. "The little dog at the bottom has no head!"

"That's right. Degas here used an unexpected compositional device. He was inspired by Japanese prints—then quite fashionable—as well as new photographic techniques making it possible to capture the fleeting instant. The little dog is depicted at the very moment he's leaving

the room! But let's all keep trying to figure out why the critics were so harsh," proposed William.

"The father turns his back to us!"

"And the mother seems so sad. She doesn't smile and she looks at no one."

"The little girl is fidgeting in her chair!"

Myself, I thought her little leg was too thin and hung down like a doll's. But I couldn't make myself heard. Theodore, our scribe, was taking notes.

"In short," concluded William, "it's as though no one posed for this portrait; it's as though Degas captured a passing moment of family life."

Portrait of the Bellelli Family, 1858–1867. Oil on canvas, 6 feet 7 inches × 8 feet 2 inches.

The following Wednesday, it was the battle of the ancients and the moderns in the studio. William had placed several books about Degas on the table. We were free to look through them for ideas. It wasn't long before disagreements broke out.

"Degas goes too far!" said Laura with irritation. "Look! Such a blatant error can't be a virtue!"

She seemed to have a point. In this painting Degas had cut off the dancers' heads!

"Apparently he wasn't all that crazy about them!" Theodore said ironically.

"It's the prettiest part of the painting, with the blue and pink touches on the tutus."

"It's true!" said Charlotte. "Soon he'd stop painting sad people and turn to dancers, the theater . . ."

"And horses!" added Oliver.

"These musicians aren't sad!" interjected Leopold, who was speaking up for the first time. "The bassoonist with his cheeks puffed out is great! That must be what happens when he plays."

"How would you know?"

"I play the trumpet in an orchestra."

"And are you as serious as that?" laughed Oliver.

Myself, I thought the dancers were magnificent. But Oliver found them funny; he only liked the horses. William smiled into his beard.

"This is exactly what happened in the nineteenth century: the quarrel of the ancients and the moderns. This was the first time Degas painted the ballet," he went on. "Once again he framed the picture like a photograph. Imagine him seated in the front row of the theater. He aims his camera at the stage. What does he get? A foreground that's very clear, quite realistic, and a background of blurry tutus. The two distinct levels of depth correspond to two aspects of Degas' personality at this moment: one part of him was still classic and dark, another was seduced by the bright, fantastic world of the dance. But he shows himself to be a remarkable portraitist here: each figure is in a familiar, typical pose. All his art is in this painting: the precision of gesture and the impressionist way with color."

The Orchestra of the Opera, 1870. Oil on canvas, 1 foot 10 inches × 1 foot 6 inches. In the foreground is Desire Dihau, bassoonist in the opera orchestra, who was close to Degas and was the painting's first owner.

"Make portraits of people in familiar and typical attitudes, above all give them faces consistent with their bodies."

We'd talked a lot about photographs and framing. William asked us to bring some vacation pictures next Wednesday. Some kids brought their cameras. Oliver's had a zoom lens with which he'd taken an astonishing photo of his dog's head.

"Soon I'll start to do horses!" he announced.

"And why not dancers?" asked Charlotte.

"You need a flash for artificial light."

Traveler's camera, circa 1880.

Corps de ballet dancer. Photographic print on glass by Degas, circa 1896.

"I should tell you, Leopold, that Degas didn't begin to take photos until 1889! Rapid exposure photography had just appeared on the scene, but Degas preferred to use an old-fashioned apparatus with a tripod and large plates; poses had to be long for the light to enter and register on the plates, which weren't as sensitive as our film today. Degas made his friends hold complicated poses for 15 minutes so he could get the light effects he wanted! For interior scenes, he lit his models with oil lamps or candles."

"They look like ghosts!"

Portable American apparatus, 1869.

19

"In the past, and even pretty recently, you had to adjust the exposure time, the aperture, the distance, and make allowances for clouds in the sky and unwanted movement. Now, all you usually have to do is push the button!"

"And frame properly," said Theodore.

"Well, yes . . . But Degas had apparently decided to frame 'improperly.'"

"How's that?"

Leopold showed us a picture of his little sister but all you could see was a piece of her dress next to a bit of grass. That didn't seem much like Degas! His kind of unusual framing was intentional; it was a matter of skill and judgement, not of error.

"Look carefully."

William opened an art book on the table. We saw a painting in which a large vase of flowers took up most of the space. The woman who had just arranged them was leaning on a small corner of the table to the right, as if she'd been pushed to the side.

"That was done on purpose!" explained William. "To underline the importance of the bouquet. And to increase our interest in the figure and her remarkably natural pose."

Woman Leaning Near a Vase of Flowers, erroneously called *Woman with Chrysanthemums,* 1865. Oil on canvas, 2 feet 5 inches × 3 feet.

"And this one?" said Heloise suddenly, who up to then hadn't seemed very interested in painting.

She had discovered in the book a little girl called Hortense Valpincon.

"Her parents were close friends of Degas. They lived in Normandy and often invited him to spend weekends with them," William told us. "One day Degas decided to do a portrait of Hortense. But a few problems arose. The painter wanted to represent her holding a piece of apple. But to pass the time the girl ate it, irritating Degas. In the end, several posing sessions were required."

"The bit of apple is in the middle of the painting!"

"That's right! And the carpet with its floral motif takes up a lot of space, just like the flowers in the other work. I don't need to tell you that the supporters of classic art didn't like what they saw . . ."

Little Hortense had kept us longer than usual in the studio. But we weren't going to ignore such a fine opportunity for taking photos of each other! We wanted to put William in every one of them.

*Portrait of Hortense
Valpincon*, 1871. Oil on
canvas, 2 feet 6 inches
× 3 feet 8 inches.

Racehorses before the Stands, 1866–1868. Essence (oil diluted with turpentine) on paper mounted on canvas, 1 foot 6 inches × 2 feet.

It was time to talk about horses.

"Let's let Oliver choose a painting," said William.

He settled on no less than four!

"Let's look at the first one, which dates from about 1868. Doesn't it already show signs of the new tendency and seem a bit 'impressionist'?" asked William.

After what we'd learned, it wasn't too difficult for us to identify a few characteristics of the new way of painting.

"Well, it's outside," Laura began.

"Very good! The atmosphere is summery and full of light," William continued.

"And the same range of colors is used everywhere, from the earth to the sky."

I was rather proud of my insight. So

was William, who then drew our attention to the vivid notes of color in the jockeys seen from the back.

"And the restless horse in the background! Maybe Degas photographed him before drawing him," said Oliver.

"You might think so. But remember that it was only later, towards 1880, that Degas encountered the work of the great British photographer Muybridge, who specialized in photographs of moving horses. Degas' gift for observation and rapid draftsmanship are more to the point here. Horses and dancers were his favorite subjects because they allowed him to show movement."

I tried to make a few little sketches, but I have to say that my horses need work! It's true that we don't see them so much any more. Nowadays we go to ball games on Sundays, not to the races.

Oliver told us he'd taken riding lessons over the summer.

"Don't laugh, but I almost like horses better than people!"

"We'll soon be seeing some," promised William.

"If we're going to the races, I'll have to get hold of a hat!" Charlotte confided to me.

Part of the crowd at the Longchamp racecourse towards the end of the nineteenth century.

We didn't go to the races, but we did go to the park at Saint Cloud. There were lots of people promenading, groups of children organizing races, and—on the narrow paths under the trees—horseback riders! Oliver tried to take pictures of horses at full gallop. "Even when they stop, it's not so easy", I said to myself, thinking about drawing them. I'd explained to an affable rider that I worked for a newspaper.

"We're all in the park this afternoon! Reporters, editors, and artists . . ."

He'd be well advised to hold that pose, if he wanted to make a good impression in our sports paper! Afterwards he gave me his card so I could send him a copy. Was I up to the challenge? I didn't 'capture' him very well, but he'd surely find some consolation in seeing the drawing by Degas that I'd use instead of mine! I was realizing how hard it was to sketch a horse. It seems Degas had very sharp eyes capable of seeing all points of view.

"He made notes as precise as 'the right hoof leaves the earth first,' " William informed us.

Rapid Movement Studies. **Brown ink, 10 inches × 8 inches.**

Suddenly Leopold wanted to ask a rider to slow down . . . but the horse didn't understand! What he needed was a circus horse. While we were making our scientific observations, Laura, sitting on the grass, was writing her own impressions. She should be left alone. But where were Leopold, Sarah, and Heloise? Night had begun to fall without our realizing it.

"Hello! Hello!" William cried in every direction.

No answer. But the suspense didn't last long. Laura saw the three of them in the distance, trying to make sense of a mysterious paper they'd found on the ground:

> *My first was a king*
> *My second was a corporal*
> *All of us were crowned emperor.*

"We'll answer the riddle in our paper!" William decided.

In front of us the first lights of the Paris evening were beginning to come on.

Eight days later, we all tiptoed into the studio . . .

"Silence!" insisted William. "We are in the dance class at the opera, on Peletier Street, in May of 1872. The rehearsal is about to begin. In a moment, the ballet master will give the signal. The atmosphere is solemn in this impressive room with its marble pilasters. Is the young dancer going to properly execute her arabesque to the rear? Very likely, because the position of her feet is perfect, and perfectly captured by Degas' 'flash' a fraction of a second before she begins to move. Let's examine the room. To the left, dancers are exercising at the barre while awaiting their turn. Standing along the length of the wall, the others prepare to assess their friend's performance."

"Another one is disappearing behind the half-open door," whispered Sarah.

Myself, I'd noticed the one looking out the window, waiting for the end of the hour. Beside me, Charlotte was trying to imitate the dancer seated on the chair. It wasn't so easy!

"Did you notice how pretty the light is?" sighed Laura.

"Somebody left a little chair in the middle of the room," Heloise remarked suddenly.

"No!" said Theodore, wrinkling his nose under his glasses. "That's the set!"

I guess he read a lot, for it seemed to me he was right.

"Just a moment, Mr. Ballet Master!"

William explained to us that the little chair served to furnish the space. Degas often used very simple objects in this way, omitting them and putting them back into the composition several times before reaching a decision. His perfec-

tionism sometimes bordered on mania. Degas painted all his ballet scenes on the basis of sketches made at the opera. Once in his studio, he assembled them like the pieces of a puzzle. It was said of him that "he observed without painting and painted without observing." In contrast to the impressionists, who painted "from the motif," which is to say directly after nature.

But be quiet! The ballet master is giving the signal. Look, the ballerina is beginning her variation.

Dance Class at the Opera, 1872. Oil on canvas, 1 foot 1 inch × 1 foot 6 inches.

"It's quite fine to copy what one sees; but it's much better to draw what one sees only in memory . . . Then your memories and your fantasy are liberated from the tyranny exercised by nature."

On our own, we found another dance class that we liked even better! Farewell to rigor: here things were more relaxed. The dancers let their attention wander from the old master leaning on his cane.

"Wouldn't it be fun to act out this painting? Why don't we surprise William!"

The girls were the most enthusiastic. Theodore put himself in charge, saying he'd already read the scenario in the book. Oliver wanted to be the dancing master. Leopold offered to take charge of the music.

"Stop playing when the curtain rises!" ordered Theodore, who didn't care for the trumpet. "Because the class is over!"

"And you, Damian?" asked Heloise.

"I'll be Degas!"

There was no objection. I draw the best!

Everything was ready the next Wednesday when William arrived at the studio. A signal was given and the trumpet rang out for a brief moment.

"Goodness, I'm tired!" began Oliver, leaning on a big stick he'd found in the woods. "At my age, still directing dance class! They're very noisy today."

"Ow!" cried Charlotte. "There's a flea on my back! Finally I can scratch! It's about time. This class is endless."

"It sure is hot!" said Laura, catching her breath and fanning herself. "Who wants to be inside in such beautiful weather?"

She was quite something with the bows in her hair and at her waist, and especially with the fan she'd brought from her parents' showcase.

The Dance Class, 1873–
1876. Oil on canvas, 2
feet 9 inches × 2 feet 6
inches.

Detail of *The Dance Class*.

All this time Heloise and Sarah were trying to move about on pointe, their feet twisted.

"Come in, Mr. Degas!" Oliver then said. "Make yourself at home. You won't disturb us. But the class is over, you've arrived too late."

"Not at all. I'm also very much interested in sketching the dancers at their ease."

"Are you going to play the big bad wolf, Mr. Degas?"

"Have no fear," I coughed out. "I'll slip into this corner with my drawing notebook. Forget about me and do whatever you like."

They started to clown around.

"Bravo!" screamed William, gathering up the props. "I congratulate you. Did you know that Degas imitated each dancer's gesture in order to draw it better? He was a superb mimic! Have you seen how his art has evolved in this painting? There are many more colors to underline details, and light is beginning to blur the shapes. The draftsman is giving way to the colorist."

Then, since we were so fond of games, William proposed a contest for the most surprising Degas.

Let's see what we came up with.

Sketch of a dancer.

The Racecourse,
Amateur Jockeys, 1877–
1880. Oil on canvas,
2 feet 2 inches × 2 feet
8 inches.

Degas certainly was an original . . .

We found lots of paintings that were unexpected in one way or another. So William decided the first prize would go to the one that was defended the best. We drew straws. The first to speak would be Oliver, who immediately went to the podium.

"Ladies and Gentlemen! This afternoon at Longchamp we will witness the famous Grand Prix, with 14 horses. Island Proverb, a very fine animal, is the favorite. He's given a slight edge over Woodland Highness. But there are other serious contenders: Alouette of the Loir, Mysterious, To Distraction, and Grand Vizir. The outcome is far from clear. At

the edge of the village a crowd has gathered along the course. Some Parisians didn't want to miss the event! You can see them in the right foreground, in elegant clothes and hats. The image was caught a bit late, which makes for the surprising framing with its fragmentary carriage wheels and severed bodies. On the other hand, the cameraman seems fascinated by the train passing through the landscape. Island Proverb looks to be in great form. Grand Vizir, with the black coat, sprained his ankle. He's resting in the foreground mounted by a jockey in a red shirt. There! I hope this television image from 1887 got through to you!" concluded Oliver, beaming.

We had all bet on Island Proverb or Mysterious, as if we were there.

"Very good!" judged William. "Oliver has shown us how contemporary this painting feels. With its vivacity and instantaneous quality, it could be from a sports show on T.V. All we have to do is replace the carriage with a car. This is one of Degas' most original works, combining superb organization with great fantasy."

Myself, I was preparing another surprise! Degas didn't spend all his time at the races or the opera. He also went to cafés, where he encountered some very unusual people. William let me take a book home, and I had fun doing imitations, just as Degas had done before he began to paint.

The winning horses in the Grand Prix de Paris, as depicted by V.J. Cotlisen.

Salvator
1875

Sᵗ Christophe . 1877

When the day came I arrived at the studio with a bowler hat over one ear, a pipe, and wearing my old tennis shoes. Sarah helped me stage the painting. Her older sister had lent her a funny hat and an evening dress. When the others arrived we were already seated at a small table with a coke and a lemonade, looking . . . weary.

"What's the matter with them?" they asked. "Are they sick?"

"I wonder," Sarah began, "if I should bother to drink this. It doesn't make me any happier!"

"Myself," I grumbled between my teeth, "I find it's the best way to forget my wretched life."

"I've seen those two somewhere before," said Charlotte. "They're not as pretty as the dancers."

"There are lots of things in Paris besides dancers!"

". . . and horse races are only on Sunday."

"But during the week Degas went to the cafe. He found his painter friends there, and also people without luck or money, like these two."

There was no stopping Theodore! Soon everybody had recognized *The Absinthe Drinker*.

"Poverty and despair often led people in this period to alcoholism," explained William. "But these two characters aren't drunks. They're two of the painter's friends, an actress and a print maker, who were willing to pose for him. Did you know that Degas made no preparatory drawings for this painting? The off-kilter composition and tables without legs help establish the loneliness and melan-

The Café de l'Empereur, near the Opera.

36

In a Café, also known as
The Absinthe Drinker,
1875–1876. Oil on
canvas, 3 feet × 2 feet 3
inches.

choly of these people in the corner of a
cafe. What an audacious painter! In this
case he was attacked not only for his
compositional daring but also for the
shocking subject matter."

Before the drawing class got started,
Oliver took a picture of our little scene
for our newspaper.

Miss Lala at the Cirque Fernando, 1879. Oil on canvas, 3 feet 10 inches × 2 feet 6 inches.

Degas wrote several sonnets about her, one of which includes the line: "Equilibrate, balance both your flight and your weight."

When it was Leopold's turn to present his painting, we were a little puzzled at first. He mounted the podium in shorts with an odd collection of props: a sack of oranges, a hoop, and a Christmas garland around his neck.

"Can you guess who I am?"

"A magician!" cried Charlotte.

"That's close!" answered Leopold, pretending to swallow the garland as he pulled it out of his sleeve.

As a magician's trick, it wasn't much. When nobody said anything, Leopold started to juggle . . . until his three oranges crashed to the ground. Then he launched into the next number by rolling the hoop between the tables. That wasn't easy to manage, either! Then, all of a sudden, he crouched down and leaped up at the curtain rod. It was the finale! But William became concerned and cried out:

"Enough of this circus!"

Leopold stopped in his tracks. William had hit on the answer. We were supposed to be at the circus.

From the back of the room we heard the small voice of Heloise, who said:

"It's Miss Lala! I saw her in one of the books."

Leopold didn't look like a girl, but with a reproduction in front of us we were convinced. *Miss Lala at the Cirque Fernando* was really a dancer who worked on the ceiling, something Leopold hadn't managed to do! All the same, William, who'd calmed down and was smiling, praised Leopold's imagination.

Decidedly, Degas was determined to take in all of Parisian life! He said it was "rich in marvellous, poetic subjects." He had the eye of a good reporter who missed nothing and who was always looking for an original angle. He didn't hesitate to show the ceiling of the circus building from an odd perspective, to capture the view of a spectator looking at Miss Lala! And he succeeded; it almost gave us vertigo! And all to make us dream—of a bird in flight, a performing acrobat suspended high above the ground.

The Cirque Fernando, study.

It was Laura's and Charlotte's turn to dazzle us . . . by inviting us to a marionette show! They'd been painting, sewing, and assembling all week.

The curtain rose on a clearing in the middle of the forest. When the music started, the little marionettes appeared one by one behind the trees and danced into the light. They spun around in their tiny gauze skirts and gracefully lifted their arms over their heads. Above, the two ballet masters pulled the strings, controlling their jumps and arabesques— and avoiding collisions! The figures circled around the stage for the finale, and the performance ended. The spotlights dimmed. The little troupe disappeared behind the wings, where a mysterious figure was hiding. Was it Degas? Alone on the stage now, the star dancer moved towards her adoring public. It's a good thing she was restrained by strings, for in her enthusiasm she almost fell into our arms.

At the intermission William asked:

"In your opinion, what is the title of this work? *The Star*? *Dancer with a Bouquet Bowing*? *Falling Dancer*?"

Of course, only a "star" would have allowed Degas to capture this artificial light he so loved.

Ballet, also known as *The Star*, 1876–1877. Pastel, 1 foot 11 inches × 1 foot 4 inches.

"I'm called the painter of female dancers. It's not understood that dancers have been for me a pretext for painting pretty materials and capturing movement."

And now, silence! The curtain rose a second time.

The set was gone. There was only a single dancer on the stage. She certainly wasn't a star! Rather a little girl taking dance class. She resembled Charlotte.

Arms in the air! Feet in first position! Arms behind the back! Feet in second position!

"Very interesting!" whispered Theodore.

Oliver thought so, too.

"You feel the muscles working like those of a horse."

Coming from him, that was quite a compliment!

Sarah throught she had big knees and a nose stuck up in the air. She was funny, this marionette.

"Her tutu is all wrinkled!" noted Heloise.

The little dancer mounted a base and stopped moving (more or less): she'd been turned into a statue!

The curtain fell.

"Why of course! She's a sculpture!" said William.

"The Little Fourteen-Year-Old Dancer!" I'm the one who identified it.

"Degas completed it in 1870. She's made of wax and dressed like a doll with a real short dress, real dance slippers, and a real bow in her hair," explained William.

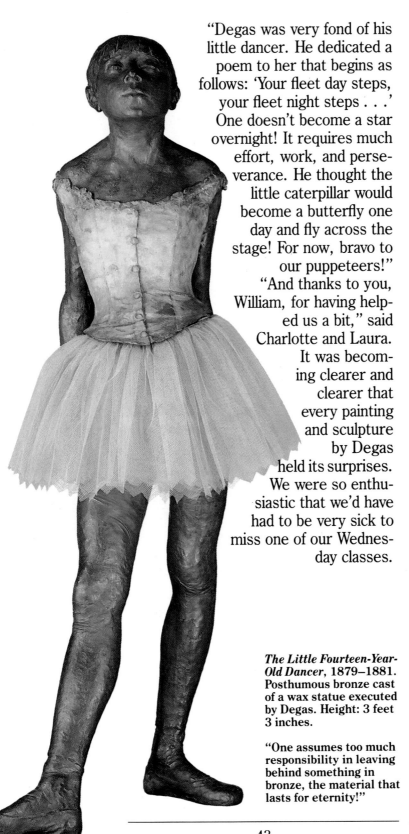

"Degas was very fond of his little dancer. He dedicated a poem to her that begins as follows: 'Your fleet day steps, your fleet night steps . . .' One doesn't become a star overnight! It requires much effort, work, and perseverance. He thought the little caterpillar would become a butterfly one day and fly across the stage! For now, bravo to our puppeteers!"

"And thanks to you, William, for having helped us a bit," said Charlotte and Laura. It was becoming clearer and clearer that every painting and sculpture by Degas held its surprises. We were so enthusiastic that we'd have had to be very sick to miss one of our Wednesday classes.

The Little Fourteen-Year-Old Dancer, **1879–1881. Posthumous bronze cast of a wax statue executed by Degas. Height: 3 feet 3 inches.**

"One assumes too much responsibility in leaving behind something in bronze, the material that lasts for eternity!"

At the Milliner's, 1882.
Pastel, 2 feet 7 inches ×
2 feet 9 inches.

"We're in the early 1880s," continued William. "Edgar Degas has become a famous painter. But he flees the world and avoids the famous salons. He contents himself with exhibiting a few works at a dealer's from time to time, when the Parisian critics all publish reviews. But he remains cloistered in his studio. He now has few friends. He reads a great deal. And he continues to take walks in the streets of his neighborhood. Look at these two pretty women! They're trying on hats without suspecting that behind the counter a sharp eye is taking them in. With a few strokes, the painter captured for us these natural gestures in front of the mirror: 'Do you think it suits me?' 'Yes, my dear, it suits you perfectly!' "

But as usual, Degas took a long time to work up the color, making it more and more sumptuous. He gradually abandoned oils for pastels, which were easier on his eyes and were ideal for rendering the texture of silk, feathers, satin, and straw. "What's more, this technique makes it possible for me to paint and draw at the same time . . . My dream!" he explained to Mary Cassatt, who'd kindly agreed to pose for him.

She was herself an artist and very much admired Degas.

"Did they get married?" asked Heloise.

"No. They were very fond of each other, but they were both very independent. And then Degas had consecrated his life to painting."

Degas in the late 1890s.

And us? What if we tried out different painting techniques in the studio? We threw ourselves into this challenge joyfully, everyone expressing himself in a way consistent with his character.

It seems Degas sometimes mixed watercolor, oil, and pastel with his fingers, something I made a point of trying. He also applied successive layers, to create an effect of relief.

Degas was in love with Paris. After a brief sojourn in Louisiana with his mother's family, he was happy to return home. "I no longer want to see anything but my own little corner, and work it devotedly," he said.

He tirelessly walked the streets of Montmartre and the neighborhood known as the Marais. There he met craftsmen and families of workers. The doors onto the stairs are open.

"Your shirt will soon be ready, Mr. Degas! Wait just a moment, please."

Mr. Degas sits on a stool and takes in the scene attentively. Sometimes he takes a small drawing pad out of his pocket and his nervous charcoal flies across the pages. But all this steam! He has to stop to wipe his glasses. Especially given that his sight is growing worse.

One good pass with the iron is all he needs to see. The gestures of these women ironers hold no secrets for him. He can mimic them like a professional!

"He could almost have ironed his shirt himself!" suggested Oliver, interrupting William's description of the scene. It was his turn to mount the boards! We had fun watching him struggle, pretending to spit on the hot iron!

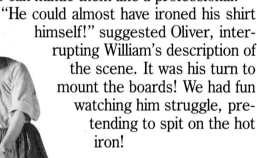

Woman ironers at the end of the nineteenth century.

"The contemporary reviewers," he explained, "criticized him for using these poor women to make paintings like others used them to iron their shirts."

It's true that they seemed very tired. The one holding a bottle of water was yawning with her mouth wide open! She'd have made us sleepy if William hadn't gotten us to laugh so hard!

This one was an oil painting, but it

Women Ironing, 1884–1886. Oil on canvas, 2 feet 6 inches × 2 feet 8 inches.

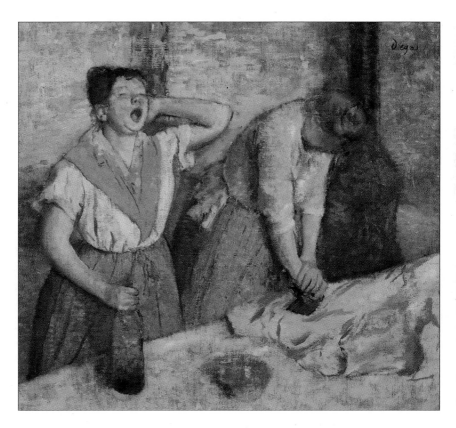

looked like pastel. Clever Degas! He had more than one trick up his sleeve.

Do you know that William had kept a record of all our meetings and retained all our drawings? It looked like the newspaper was going to be terrific!

The Singer in Green,
circa 1884. Pastel, 2 feet
× 1 foot 6 inches.

It was such a beautiful day that we decided to go for a walk in Montmartre, the neighborhood of artists. William told us that each of its streets had a story— that of an artist who'd lived there or a poet who'd sung its praises. Vincent Van Gogh had lived on Lepic Street. Degas on Laval Street and then in turn on Blanche Street, Frocot Street, Victor Masse Street, and finally Clichy Boulevard. Now, even though their names and appearance have changed and artists no

longer live on these streets, the pictur-
esque atmosphere remains. Poets gathered at the Black Cat, a local club. At
other such spots one could hear the sing-
ing of Aristide Bruant, while the famous
performers Valentin le Desosse and La
Goulue could be seen at the Moulin
Rouge.

Now we were treated to Oliver the
frizzy, Theodore with glasses, red-
cheeked Charlotte, and Laura-Laura.
"And when the Spring comes again . . ."
The eight of us made as much noise as a
bus full of tourists. There was also a real
600-year-old windmill at the top of the
hill. Degas adored Montmartre, which
offered something like rustic calm at the
edge of the city. He wandered its streets,
on the lookout for arresting scenes. As
for us, we didn't find any ironers. There
weren't many milliners either, and their
hats were much less fancy. But at night
the cabarets still ring with song.

"Without going to a café-concert, we'll
become acquainted with the singer in
green," William announced to us that day.
"Just looking at her puts you in the
mood!"

"Can you hear her sing?" asked Laura,
murmuring through her teeth. "Timela,
Lamelou, pan, pan, Timela, Timelamelou
. . ."

"She kind of resembles the little 14-
year-old dancer," observed Theodore.

Could it be the same model?

"In this pastel Degas obtained a superb
effect by superimposing the colors of the
singer's dress. Don't forget that she sang
in Montmartre and not at the opera!" said
William.

And suddenly he went to get his guitar.

"Do you know any of the hit songs from 1880–1900? "When she was little, at night, she went to Saint Margaret . . . At the Bastille everyone loves Nini the dog-skinned! She's so good and so kind . . ." Plunk! Plunk! "Ta-ma-ra boom di-ay, Just dance and try to stay gay, For that's the only way, To keep your troubles at bay!" Plunk! Plunk! "Around the Black Cat I'm on the prowl, By the moonlight in Montmartre . . ." Plunk! Plunk! went the guitar.

William knew an entire repertory, and we soon learned it ourselves. Sometimes the words were a bit old-fashioned. We didn't always completely understand them. But we had a terrific time, as if we were at a café-concert. Like Degas; but Degas was becoming less and less happy, more and more solitary. He was afraid of going blind.

Even so, he continued to paint in the silence of his studio. Color now prevailed in his work, but the movements of dancers and women at their toilette were still captured with his usual precision.

We decided to return to the Orsay Museum, which now seemed as familiar to us as a house full of memories of people we'd known, the artists who were showing us so much about the world. We looked forward to rediscovering Degas and his most beautiful pastels, shown in reduced light to protect them, and to see them up close, the real things . . .

It was a bit mysterious in the semi-darkness. It made us want to keep our voices low.

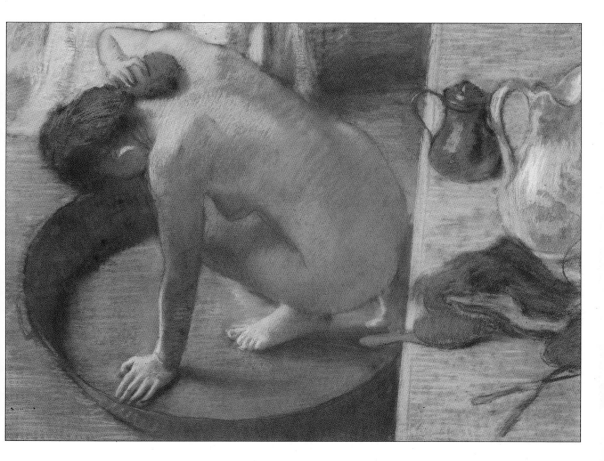

"What a peculiar little tub," whispered Charlotte. "It looks like a plate!"

"Yes," said Theodore. "There's one like it in my grandmother's attic, but I wouldn't want to bathe in it."

Thinking about that made us laugh. But the pastel bather had as much grace as a dancer.

"What always interests Degas," William explained, "is capturing a woman's posture. Here, it's the movement of her arm over her shoulder and the gesture of her hand pressing the sponge, and then the exact placement of the rest of her body at that precise moment."

It seems Degas went about his work very scientifically!

Woman Bathing in a Shallow Tub, **1886. Pastel, 2 feet × 2 feet 9 inches.**

Degas doesn't flatter women; what interests him in these nudes is the movement of their limbs, the posture of their bodies. He himself said: "Perhaps I considered women too much like animals."

"And what's more, the modeling is perfect; in other words, thanks to a balance between the fine drawing and the color rendering all the nuances of the skin, the painting has relief like a sculpture."

Looking at the work up close, we could see the vertical and horizontal strokes that created this effect of relief.

"There must be hot water in the copper pitcher and cold water in the glass one," said Laura. "And look at the two brushes."

"Accessories in the foreground!" asserted Oliver with authority. "He's like a film director, this Degas!"

"Exactly! Note the plunging perspective of the cameraman, who sees the bather from above. Degas is a precursor of future tendencies in painting—of cubism, for example. He understood the rich potential of combining several image fragments like no other painter of his time."

Woman Bathing in a Shallow Tub, details. This work is one of seven pastels on this theme realized by Degas in the 1880s.

We had only to turn around to see a figure that was still more modern, a woman combing her hair.

"Bands of color shape the woman's sculptural body and swirl in the background. The contours are vigorous, the line quite simple. There are few accessories. The eye is persistently drawn to the long hair and the comb. The broad strokes over the body make it seem like stone! A sculpture!" said William, growing more and more excited.

"It's as though she were playing the cello!" said Heloise in her small voice.

"Degas here uses a new range of luxuriant, vivid colors: electric blue, pink, yellow, purple . . . The young painter Gauguin would say that Degas had rediscovered the nude. In effect, all his large pastel nudes are in a new classic style based on line. At this moment of his life, Degas is drawing on the sum total of his experience and paints almost always from memory. His failing eyes no longer allow him to copy what he sees. In this way he gradually abandons humor, anecdote, and all insignificant details in favor of line, volume, and color."

Myself, I saw that this woman's face was painted in green, blue, and orange! A bit unusual? And yet it seemed very natural. What if I tried something similar? A self portrait, so the others won't be annoyed if it isn't good.

Woman Combing Her Hair, 1890–1892. Pastel, 2 feet 9 inches × 1 foot 10 inches.

"Ah! Where is the time when I believed myself strong, when I was full of projects? I'll very quickly head down the incline and roll I don't know where, enveloped in lots of bad pastels like so much wrapping paper."

"Look!" Leopold cried. "The bather in her tub!"

It was indeed her, but she'd changed position.

"She's relaxing in her saucer!" said Oliver, laughing.

"Just think that originally she had a real sponge in her hand!" William told us. To give his sculpture a realist character, Degas also used a mixture of red wax, plaster, lead, and even wood. It was more faithful to the colors of the flesh. But the work was so fragile that it was hard for a founder to make a bronze cast of it."

In fact, Degas didn't like casts to be made from his wax statues. He just wanted to knead and model the wax as he pleased. Under his fingers, the unexpected was always possible! The experience interested him more than the final product.

The Tub, series P no. 26.
Height: 8 inches.
Bronze.

A detail of the de Gas family gravesite in the Montmartre cemetery.

At the end of his life, all that remained for him was this ability to create. "If you'd given me a hat full of diamonds, it wouldn't have made me as happy as destroying this work and starting all over again", Degas once said to his friend Ambroise Vollard, the picture dealer. Despite the artist's age and infirmity, these rapidly executed statuettes are full of strength and announce twentieth century Expressionism.

Degas died in 1917, during World War I, at the age of 83, and was buried in the family plot in Montmartre cemetery.

"I don't want any funeral oration, just let it be said simply over my grave: he was very fond of drawing."

The time had passed too quickly! We didn't want to separate from one another. But we still had several days work ahead of us to pull together our newspaper. We had lots of ideas, photos, and reproductions. Our studio had come to resemble a museum! Perhaps we should think about giving tours! As soon as the paper was published, William was so proud that he took it to show people at the museum. The real one!

One of the curators was very interested in our project. She congratulated us on our study of Degas, who by now seemed like a personal friend. But then, it's well known he had a gift for making children laugh.

GLOSSARY

absinthe: a bitter, green alcoholic drink.

Black Cat: night club in the Montmartre section of Paris frequented by Degas and his friends.

Cassatt, Mary: American painter (1845–1926) who resettled permanently in Paris in the 1870s, befriending many impressionist artists of the day.

Expressionism: a movement in art orginating in the late 19th and early 20th centuries emphasizing the feelings and inner experiences of the painter.

Grand Prix: the forerunner of today's famous international automobile race of the same name; during the time of Degas, the Grand Prix was the most celebrated horse race in Paris.

Marais, the: neighborhood in central Paris known for its quiet streets and elegant town houses.

The Little Dancer advertising a dance performance at the Opera.

The Paris Opera.

Montmartre: neighborhood in the hilly, northern part of Paris known for its nightclubs and cabarets, the beautiful Church of the Sacred Heart, and the city's largest collection of street painters.

Moulin Rouge, The: famous nightclub in the Montmartre section of Paris.

Paris: The city of lights, Paris is the capital and largest city of France; commonly regarded as the art and fashion center of the world.

The entrance to the White Street metro.

The Moulin Rouge.

Chronology

1834:	Birth on July 19, of Hilaire Germain Edgar de Gas, at no. 8 rue Saint-Georges in Paris. His father, a banker, was from Naples. His mother belonged to a Creole family from New Orleans.
1845–1853:	Attends the Lycee Louis-le-Grand in Paris.
1847:	Death of his mother.
1852:	Thanks to his father, meets some of the great collectors of the period, among them Edouard Valpincon.
1853:	Attends law school.
1853–1855:	Studies at Barrias' studio, then with a student of Ingres. Enters the Ecole des Beaux-Arts.
1856–1859:	Trip to Italy. Begins *Portrait of the Bellelli Family*.
1860–1861:	Portraits and historical subjects. First studies of horses and riders.
1862:	Begins a long friendship with Manet, who introduces him to Renoir, Monet, and Zola.
1864:	Executes several portraits of Manet.
1865:	Exhibits at the Salon. Changes his signature to "Degas".
1865–1870:	Executes a series of portraits, first single figures and then groups.
1866:	*The Steeplechase* (*The Wounded Jockey*) is shown at the Salon.
1868:	Becomes interested in the theater.
1870–1872:	Degas fights in the war with Prussia; is in Normandy during the Commune. He begins to have vision problems and avoids painting in bright light. First represents dancers at the opera.
1872:	Meets Durand-Ruel, the celebrated dealer.
1872–1873:	Travels to New Orleans.
1874:	Death of his father. Exhibits 10 works in the first Impressionist exhibition.
1875:	Italian journey: visits Naples, Florence, Pisa, and Genoa.
1876:	Second Impressionist exhibition; he exhibits 24 works, including *In a Café*. First depictions of the cafe-concert.
1877:	Third Impressionist exhibition; he exhibits 22 prints, drawings, monotypes, and canvases.
1878:	Progressively abandons oils for pastels.
1879:	Fourth Impressionist exhibition; exhibits fans, portraits, and *Miss Lala at the Cirque Fernando*.
1879–1880:	Exhibits prints with Mary Cassat and Camille Pissarro.
1880:	Travels in Spain. Completes his first sculpture, of a schoolgirl.
1881:	Participates in the sixth Impressionist exhibition with several pastels and a near life-size wax statue, *The Little Fourteen-Year-Old Dancer*.
1882:	Degas does not participate in the seventh Impressionist exhibition. Several pastels of milliners' shops. Takes up once more the theme of women ironing. First important works representing women at their toilette. Short trip to Spain, then a sojourn near Geneva.
1884:	Spends the summer in the Orne with his friends the Valpincons.
1885:	Trip to Le Havre, Mont Saint-Michel, and Dieppe, where he meets Gauguin.
1886:	January in Naples. Last Impressionist exhibition. Contract with Durand-Ruel.